P9-DHJ-702

Child's Guide to Baptism

SUE STANTON

ILLUSTRATIONS BY ANNE CATHARINE BLAKE

Paulist Press
New York/Mahwah, N.J.

To my parish family of St. Cecilia's Church
SS
For Anais, Zoey, and Amalie Henze
ACB

Excerpts from the English translation of *Rite of Baptism for Children* © 1969, International Committee on English in the Liturgy, Inc. All rights reserved.

Caseside design by Sharyn Banks
Caseside illustration by Anne Catharine Blake

Library of Congress Cataloging-in-Publication

Stanton, Sue, 1952-
    Child's guide to baptism / Sue Stanton ; illustrations by Anne Catharine Blake.
        p. cm.
    Includes bibliographical references.
    ISBN 0-8091-6728-X (alk. paper)
    1. Baptism—Catholic Church—Juvenile literature. I. Blake, Anne Catharine. II. Title.
    BX2205.S73 2006
    264'.02081—dc22

2005032901

Published by Paulist Press
997 Macarthur Boulevard
Mahwah, New Jersey 07430

www.paulistpress.com

Printed and bound in Mexico

Hello. My name is Anthony. I've been waiting for you. I want to show you something so special it happens only once in a person's life. It's called BAPTISM and today my new baby brother is being baptized.

Come into our church and see.

What exactly is Baptism? It is the first of seven sacraments, which are signs of God's love for us.

Baptism gives us special blessings we can receive only from God. It makes us a child of God. We become a member of the huge family that is the Church, and our family can be found all over the world!

Baptism also takes away original sin, the one sin we are all born with. If we are no longer babies, it also takes away all our sins up to that minute.

We are only baptized once. Once you're in God's family, you are welcome there forever! But Baptism is just the first time we can have our sins taken away. God is always ready to forgive us.

Jesus got baptized too even though he was without sin. He wanted to show us how important it was, and so he went into the Jordan River and was baptized by John. Then he began his work of teaching, healing, and telling people about God's love. Jesus asked his followers to baptize others as well so that they could begin their own work of telling people this good news.

Shhh....We better stop talking now. Here comes Father Terry. I think he is about to start.

In our church, everyone is baptized on Sunday during Mass. It is a time when the entire congregation is gathered together. That way everyone can join in the celebration. It also reminds us that every time a Baptism is performed, that person becomes a member of our big family the Church.

Father Terry is standing next to the baptismal font. Can you find him?
"What name do you give your child?" he asks.
"James," answer my parents.

My parents chose my brother's name very carefully. He is named after a great saint. St. James was one of the apostles, the first followers of Jesus. James became a martyr for our faith in the early Church. My parents named *me* after St. Anthony of Padua. Padua is the city in Italy where St. Anthony lived.

Baptismal names are important because they can show us how to act. They can be the names of saints, who are role models, or they can be virtues like joy or patience. I am not a very patient person, so I'm glad my parents named me Anthony!

Do you know why you have the name you do?

Aunt Lucy and Uncle Mark are my brother's godparents. Godparents are very important people in the life of the newly baptized person. They support the person's family in their faith as well as in the life of the Church. They are like having a second set of parents.

Do you know the names of your godparents?

"Each of us is a child of God, thanks to our faith in Jesus Christ," says Father Terry. "All of us have a place in the one Christian family that belongs only to Christ."

Remember I told you that Baptism makes us part of a much bigger family, a huge Christian family? Another name for this family is the Mystical Body of Christ. My baby brother will soon be a part of this much bigger family. It means that he will have family all over the world, just like you and I do.

My teacher, Mrs. Bianchi, hung up a huge map in the classroom. She asked us to pick out places in the world where there are other people who are part of the Mystical Body of Christ. Then she asked us how we could show that we and they are part of the same family.

How could *you* show it?

Father Terry begins to pray again. He says, "Let us ask the help of all the saints that have gone before us marked with the sign of faith in Jesus Christ."

After Father Terry reads each name, everyone in church repeats the words, "Pray for us." I do too!

"Holy Mary, Mother of God...pray for us."

"Saint John the Baptist...pray for us."

"Saint Joseph...pray for us."

"Saint Peter and Saint Paul...pray for us."

"Saint Anthony...pray for us."

"Saint James...pray for us."

Can you think of any other saints you'd like to add? Just say "Pray for us" after it if you do.

Father Terry is holding special holy oil to bless my brother with. Both my parents and James's godparents dip their thumb into the oil and make the sign of the cross on my brother's forehead. Now it's my turn. While I make the sign of the cross, I pray to myself, *Please God, help me to be a good brother for James in his new life.*

Can you make the sign of the cross using just your thumb?

Next Father Terry says, "My dear brothers and sisters, we now ask God to give this child new life in abundance through water and the Holy Spirit."

Father Terry blesses the water that will be used to baptize James. He will pour it over my brother's head as a sign that he is being washed clean of sin. James will be a new creation. First he was born to my parents, and now he will be born into our faith and the Church.

"You have called your child, James, to this cleansing water that he may share in the faith of your Church and have eternal life. By the mystery of this consecrated water, lead him to a new spiritual birth. We ask this through Christ our Lord."

What do you think we say?

"Amen!"

I know what that word means because my Dad taught it to me. It means "so it is!" Whenever we say "Amen," we are saying that our words are the truth.

Now comes a very important moment. Mom and Dad both look nervous and very, very serious. Since James is too little to speak for himself, it is up to my parents and godparents and the whole parish—even me—to speak for him.

Father Terry asks, "Do you reject sin, so as to live in the freedom of God's children?"

"I do," I answer with everyone else, and I really mean it, too.

"Do you believe in Jesus Christ, his only Son, our Lord, who was born of the Virgin Mary, was crucified, died, and was buried, rose from the dead, and is now seated at the right hand of the Father?"

"I do."

"Do you believe in the Holy Spirit, the holy catholic Church, the communion of saints, the forgiveness of sins, the resurrection of the body, and life everlasting?"

I'm not sure what all these words mean, but I do know that with the help of my parents and godparents and teachers, someday I will learn about them. So I say, "I do."

"This is our faith. This is the faith of the Church. We are proud to profess
t, in Christ Jesus our Lord."

"Amen."

I stand up a little taller when I hear those words. It makes me feel good to know that they were said at my own Baptism. And now I can say them for myself because Baptism is forever.

Baptism calls me to be the best child of God that I can be. It calls me to love the family I live with and to love my bigger family of the Church in the world. Baptism also calls me to do both these things my whole life long.

How can *you* love the family you live with? How can *you* love your bigger family of the Church in the world?

Finally! Here is the moment we've all been waiting for.

"James, I baptize you in the name of the Father, and of the Son, and of the Holy Spirit."

Ohhh....James is so good! He doesn't even cry!

"Receive the light of Christ.

"Parents and godparents, this light is entrusted to you to be kept burning brightly. This child of yours has been enlightened by Christ. He is to walk always as a child of the light."

Can you find the big Easter candle? Uncle Mark uses it to light a special smaller candle for James. It is called a baptismal candle, and my parents will always keep it in a special place in our home.

Do you know where your baptismal candle is kept?

Father Terry blesses my mother, then my father, then everyone in the church. He ends, "May Almighty God, the Father, and the Son, and the Holy Spirit, bless you."

Father Terry gives a big smile.
"It is my privilege to introduce to you our newest member, James."
Everyone claps!

One day James will understand what the rest of our sacraments mean. Just like *I* will when I make my First Holy Communion! But until then, I have a lot to learn.

Wouldn't you like to learn with me?